SPIRITUAL WARFARE PRAYERS

MODERN EDITION

FAITHSTONE

© 2024 Faithstone LLC

For any inquiries, please contact

Faithstone LLC
1001 S Main St
Kalispell, MT 59901
Website: faithstone.org

A Word of Encouragement

The devotions in this book reflect genuine spiritual insights meant to inspire, strengthen, and deepen your walk with the Lord. While they can enrich your faith, they are not intended to stand in place of professional or pastoral care if significant challenges arise. It is always wise to seek qualified help when necessary. May these pages be a blessing to you, leading to greater hope and a closer relationship with Christ.

Trademarks

All trademarks, service marks, product names, and logos mentioned in this book are the property of their respective owners. Our mention of them is to share inspiration, not an endorsement or affiliation.

EXPERIENCE THE POWER OF PRAYER ANYTIME, ANYWHERE.

Take your prayer journey further with the **free** audio version of the prayers from this book. These calming, guided prayers are perfect for moments when you're on the go or seeking peace and connection.

- Feel inspired as each prayer is spoken with sincerity and care.
- Find peace with playlists crafted for healing, protection, and strength.
- Stay connected to God no matter where you are.

Scan the QR code below or visit **faithstone.org** to claim your **free access**.

Table of Contents

Welcome to the Battle

If you're reading this, it's not by accident. Something inside you knows there's more to life than what you can see. You've felt the tension—the fear that creeps in, the doubts that linger, the struggles that weigh you down.

What you're feeling is real. You're in a spiritual battle. But here's the good news: you've already been given the victory.

Through Jesus, you have everything you need to fight the darkness and reclaim your peace. You don't have to live in fear. You don't have to stay stuck. God has promised to protect you, to strengthen you, and to fight for you.

This book is a guide to help you step into that promise. It's filled with prayers that call on the power of God to break chains, restore hope, and bring healing.

You're stronger than you think. And with God by your side, nothing can stand against you. Let's walk into victory—together.

The Unseen War

Every day, whether you realize it or not, you're part of an invisible battle. It's not a fight against people or circumstances—it's a war fought in the spiritual realm.

The Bible tells us:

"For we do not wrestle against flesh and blood, but against the rulers, against the authorities, against the cosmic powers over this present darkness, against the spiritual forces of evil in the heavenly places."
~ Ephesians 6:12

Spiritual warfare is the ongoing struggle between God's kingdom and the forces of darkness. It's not just a grand cosmic battle—it's deeply personal. It's the tug-of-war over your thoughts, your peace, your relationships, and your purpose. While God calls you into freedom, the enemy works tirelessly to sow fear, doubt, and destruction.

The Hidden Fight

Spiritual warfare isn't always dramatic—it often shows up in the quiet moments of your life:

- That persistent feeling of fear or anxiety that steals your peace.
- The temptation to believe you're not good enough, strong enough, or loved enough.
- The doubts that creep in when life doesn't go as planned.
- The anger, bitterness, or shame that keeps you stuck in the past.

These struggles may feel overwhelming, but they're not random. The enemy's goal is to separate you from God's truth and keep you trapped in cycles of defeat. But the enemy's power is limited. As a child of God, you've already been given authority through Jesus to resist these attacks and stand firm.

How to Equip Yourself for Victory

God has not left you defenseless in this battle. In fact, He's given you everything you need to overcome. Here's how you can equip yourself for victory:

Lean on God's Strength, you are not fighting this battle alone.

"The Lord will fight for you; you need only to be still."
~ Exodus 14:14

Call on God for strength and rely on His power to guide you.

Put on the Armor of God

In Ephesians 6:10–18, Paul describes the spiritual armor God provides to protect and equip you:

The Belt of Truth to stand firm in God's promises.

The Breastplate of Righteousness to guard your heart.

The Shoes of Peace to stand firm in the gospel.

The Shield of Faith to block the enemy's attacks.

The Helmet of Salvation to protect your mind.

The Sword of the Spirit (God's Word) to fight back.

Pray Without Ceasing:
Prayer isn't just part of the battle—it's the foundation of your victory. Through prayer, you align yourself with God's will, declare His promises, and invite His power into your life.

Stay Rooted in Scripture:
God's Word is your weapon against lies and fear. When Jesus was tempted by Satan, He responded with scripture (Matthew 4:1–11). You can do the same.

Remember the Victory is Already Won:
Jesus' death and resurrection sealed the victory over sin and darkness. You're not fighting for victory—you're fighting from a place of victory.

How to Use This Book

This book is designed to be your spiritual companion—a guide for daily connection with God and a tool to help you navigate life's greatest challenges. Whether you need strength to face the day or deliverance from a specific struggle, you'll find prayers, scripture, and reflections to meet you exactly where you are.

Daily Prayers for Strength

Each day is a new opportunity to align yourself with God's presence and promises. These daily prayers are like armor—helping you face the world with courage, peace, and faith.

Morning Protection
Start your day by inviting God into your heart and asking for His protection over your mind, body, and spirit.

Suggested morning prayers: *Anima Christi* or *Psalm 91: God's Shelter and Refuge.*

Midday Reset
When the day feels heavy or distractions creep in, pause and realign yourself with God's strength. A short prayer can bring clarity and calm to any moment.

Evening Reflection
End your day by reflecting on God's faithfulness, giving thanks for His protection, and finding rest in His peace.

Organized for Your Journey

This book is divided into sections to make it easy to find the prayers that resonate with your needs. You'll find:

Protection Prayers
Foundational prayers to align yourself with Christ and shield yourself from spiritual attacks.

Prayers for Specific Struggles
Targeted prayers to guide you through challenges like fear, doubt, or loneliness.

Each section is designed to be flexible, so you can use the book in the way that works best for you—whether as a daily devotional or a resource to turn to during difficult moments.

PROTECTION IN CHRIST

No matter what challenges arise, God offers His protection to carry you through, giving you peace and strength for every step.

The Lord is my refuge and my fortress, my God,

in whom I trust.

Psalm 91:2

Anima Christi

Christ Jesus, my Savior and King,
Draw me closer into Your holy presence.
Let Your body give me life,
Your blood purify my soul,
And Your Spirit carry me in peace.

Wash over me with the waters of Your love,
And strengthen my heart with the fire of Your sacrifice.
Keep me hidden in the shadow of Your wings,
Where no evil can harm me and no fear can take hold.

Guard me from the attacks of the enemy,
And surround me with the light of Your truth.
When this journey ends, call me home to You,
Where I will rejoice forever in Your glory.

Christ, my refuge, my strength, my all—I am Yours.

Amen.

Praying Psalm 91

Heavenly Father,

I come to You, seeking refuge under Your mighty wings. You are my shelter, my fortress, and my God, in whom I place all my trust.

You deliver me from the traps of the enemy and protect me from harm. Your faithfulness surrounds me like a shield, giving me strength and peace in the face of fear.

I will not fear the terrors of the night or the dangers that come by day. Even when troubles surround me, I will stand firm, knowing that You are my defender and protector.

May Your angels lift me up and shield me from every danger. Guide my steps on the path You have set before me and keep me steady in Your care.

You are my refuge and my salvation. In Your presence, I find safety, strength, and peace. I trust in Your promises and rest in the shadow of Your almighty care.

~In Jesus' name, Amen.

Protection Against Spiritual Attacks

Heavenly Father,

I come before You, trusting in Your power and protection. You are my refuge, my defender, and my shield.

In the name of Jesus Christ, I stand against every scheme of the enemy. I bind all forces of darkness sent to harm me or distract me from Your purpose. By the authority of Christ, I declare that no weapon formed against me will prosper.

Surround me with Your light, Lord, and let Your presence drive out every shadow of fear and doubt. Guard my heart, my mind, and my spirit from the attacks of the enemy. Cover me with the power of Your truth and protect me from every lie and deception.

Lord, send Your angels to stand watch over me. Let them guard my home, my loved ones, and every step I take. Keep me steady in the face of trials and remind me that the battle belongs to You.

Thank You for being my stronghold, my Savior, and my peace. I trust in Your power to protect me and lead me into victory. *~ In Jesus' name, Amen.*

ANXIETY
AND
OVERWHELM

When anxiety takes hold, it can feel like you're carrying the weight of the world on your shoulders, leaving you exhausted and searching for relief.

Do not be anxious about anything, but in every situation, by prayer and petition, with thanksgiving, present your requests to God.

Philippians 4:6

A Prayer for Calm in the Chaos

Heavenly Father,

When the chaos of life overwhelms me, I feel the weight of anxiety pressing on my heart. It's like a storm raging inside me, leaving me restless and searching for relief. But You, Lord, are the giver of peace—the One who calms every storm and quiets every fear.

Today, I bring my fears and worries to You. I lay them at Your feet, trusting that You are greater than anything I face. Silence the noise in my mind, Lord, and fill my heart with Your steadying presence. Remind me that I am not alone, that You are with me in every moment, even when I can't feel it.

Drive out every anxious thought and replace it with Your truth. Speak Your promises over my heart—that You are my refuge, my strength, and my ever-present help. Fill me with the peace that surpasses all understanding, a peace that comes only from You.

Lord, let Your Spirit guide me and comfort me. Help me to trust You with all that I cannot control and to rest in the knowledge that You are in control. Teach me to find joy even in the chaos, knowing that Your plans for me are good.

~*In Jesus' name, Amen.*

Release Control and Trust God

Heavenly Father,

I confess that so often I try to carry burdens that are too heavy for me. I hold on to control when I should be surrendering to You, trying to fix everything in my own strength. But today, I let go. I release my need to figure everything out, and I place my worries into Your hands.

I trust that You see the bigger picture, the parts of my life that feel confusing and uncertain to me. You are good, You are faithful, and You have a plan that is greater than anything I could imagine. When my mind races, quiet my thoughts and remind me of Your promises.

Help me to lean into Your Word and Your truth. Replace my doubts with faith in Your unfailing love. Show me that even when I can't see the outcome, You are working all things for my good. Teach me to walk forward with confidence, knowing that You are holding me every step of the way.

Give me the courage to trust You in the small things and the big things. Let my surrender be an act of worship, declaring that You are my God and my hope. Thank You for carrying the weight I was never meant to bear.

~In Jesus' name, Amen.

Strength When Overwhelmed

Lord Jesus,

I come to You feeling worn out, weighed down, and overwhelmed. My heart feels heavy, my mind is restless, and the demands of life seem more than I can handle. I feel like I'm carrying a weight I wasn't meant to bear, and I don't know how to find relief. But You, Lord, are my refuge and my strength, my ever-present help in trouble.

When I feel like I'm sinking, lift me up with Your love. When I don't have the strength to move forward, carry me with Your grace. Remind me that I don't have to face this on my own—you are with me, fighting my battles and calming my fears.

Fill my heart with Your peace, the peace that quiets every storm and reassures me that I am held by You. Renew my strength, Lord, and help me to take the next step with faith, knowing that Your power is made perfect in my weakness. Teach me to trust Your timing and to rest in Your presence, even when the path ahead feels unclear.

Thank You for being my strong tower, my peace, and my unshakable hope. I rest in Your love, confident that You will sustain me through every trial.

~In Jesus' name, Amen.

LONELINESS AND ISOLATION

Feeling alone, even in a crowd, can be one of the most painful experiences. But you are never truly alone—God is always with you.

The Lord is close to the brokenhearted and saves those who are crushed in spirit.

Psalm 34:18

God's Presence in Isolation

Heavenly Father,

When loneliness surrounds me, it's easy to feel forgotten and unseen. The silence feels heavy, and the emptiness in my heart often feels too much to bear. But You, Lord, remind me that I am never alone. You are with me in the quiet moments, the hard days, and the empty spaces.

Fill my heart with the comfort of Your presence, Lord. Wrap me in Your love and remind me that I am seen, known, and cherished by You. Speak to my soul, calling me closer to You. Help me to hear Your voice and feel Your peace, even when life feels overwhelming.

Teach me to rest in the truth that I am Your child, deeply loved and never abandoned. Replace the lies of loneliness with the truth of Your unfailing companionship. Give me the strength to find joy and hope, even in the midst of solitude, knowing that You are always near.

Thank You, Lord, for being my constant companion, my greatest comfort, and the One who fills every void in my life. With You by my side, I am never truly alone.

~In Jesus' name, Amen.

Connection and Belonging

Heavenly Father,

You created us to live in connection with others, and yet I find myself feeling isolated and distant. I long for relationships that bring joy, encouragement, and love, but it often feels so difficult to find my place in the world.

Lord, I ask You to guide me toward meaningful connections. Open doors for friendships and community that reflect Your love and truth. Help me to be bold in reaching out to others, even when it feels scary or vulnerable. Teach me to trust that You will place the right people in my life at the right time.

When I feel rejected or unseen, remind me that I always belong to You. Your love fills every void in my heart, and in Your kingdom, I am never without a family. Let this truth give me confidence and peace as I walk through seasons of loneliness.

Fill my heart with Your love so completely that I can reflect it to those around me. Teach me to be a friend to others in the way You are a friend to me— unconditionally and faithfully.

Thank You for being the source of connection, belonging, and love in my life.
~In Jesus' name, Amen.

Comfort in Grief

Heavenly Father,

My heart feels heavy with grief, and the weight of loss leaves me feeling so alone. There are moments when the sadness feels overwhelming, and I don't know how to move forward. But I know that You see my pain, and You are close to me in my sorrow.

Hold me in Your arms, Lord, and comfort me with Your presence. Let me feel Your peace in the midst of my heartache and the quiet assurance that I am not walking this path alone. Wipe away my tears and remind me of the hope I have in You. You are my refuge and strength, my ever-present help in trouble.

Teach me how to carry this loss without losing hope. Help me to release my pain into Your hands, trusting that You are working even in the hardest moments. When the grief feels too much to bear, fill me with the courage to face each day and the faith to keep moving forward.

Thank You for Your unfailing love and for being the God who sees me, holds me, and walks with me. I place my sorrow in Your hands and rest in the hope that You will bring beauty from ashes.

~In Jesus' name, Amen.

ADDICTION
AND
TEMPTATION

Whether it's a habit you can't break
or a temptation that feels impossible
to resist, addiction can leave you
feeling stuck, powerless, and alone.
But God's power is greater, and His
grace is sufficient to break every
chain.

No temptation has overtaken you except what is

common to mankind. And God is faithful; he will

not let you be tempted beyond what you can

bear. But when you are tempted, he will also

provide a way out so that you can endure it.

1 Corinthians 10:13

Breaking Addictive Patterns

Heavenly Father,
You see the struggles I carry—the habits and addictions that have become chains, holding me back from the life You've called me to. They've caused pain, robbed me of peace, and left me feeling powerless to break free. But I believe in Your power to save, heal, and restore.

I renounce every hold these addictions have on me, and I bring them before You, laying them at Your feet. In Your name, I declare that these chains are broken and that they have no authority over my life. Fill the empty places in my heart and mind with Your Spirit, so there is no room for these destructive patterns to return.

Give me the courage to take each day step by step, trusting You to guide me. Surround me with people who will support me in this journey and help me to build a new foundation rooted in Your Word. Strengthen me when I feel weak, and remind me that Your grace is sufficient for me in every moment.

Lord, I trust in Your ability to transform my life and lead me into the freedom You promise. I praise You for being my strength and my refuge, my source of hope and peace.

~In Jesus' name, Amen.

Strength Against Temptation

Lord,

Temptation often feels overwhelming, like a relentless wave trying to pull me under. It comes in moments of weakness, whispering lies that draw me away from the path You've set before me. But I know that You are stronger than any temptation, and You promise to help me endure and overcome.

When temptation strikes, open my eyes to see the way out that You provide. Remind me that I am not fighting alone—you are with me, and your Spirit gives me the power to resist. Help me to stand firm in Your Word and to cling to Your promises when my will feels weak.

Give me discernment to recognize the traps of the enemy and the courage to turn away. Fill my heart with a greater desire for You than for anything else, and teach me to find satisfaction and joy in Your presence.

Lord, I pray for wisdom to make choices that honor You, even when they feel hard in the moment. Strengthen my faith and help me to see every victory over temptation as a testament to Your power working within me. Thank You for loving me through my struggles and for being my constant guide.

~In Jesus' name, Amen.

Renewal and Freedom

Heavenly Father,

I come to You longing for freedom. The struggles of my past and the habits I can't seem to break weigh me down and keep me from fully living in Your love and purpose. But I know that You have already won the victory and that You desire to make me new.

Renew my mind, Lord. Wash away the guilt and shame I've carried and replace it with the assurance of Your forgiveness and grace. Help me to let go of my past mistakes and to walk forward with confidence in the freedom You've given me.

Fill my heart with a renewed sense of joy and purpose. Teach me to trust Your plans for my life, even when they feel uncertain. Surround me with people who will encourage me and hold me accountable, and let Your Word be my guide as I take steps toward healing and restoration.

Lord, I know that this journey won't always be easy, but I trust in Your strength to carry me when I feel weak. Let every victory, big or small, remind me of Your power and love. I surrender my struggles to You, knowing that You are my freedom and my peace.

~*In Jesus' name, Amen.*

FEAR
AND
DOUBT

Fear can paralyze you, and doubt can
make you question your purpose and
God's promises. But fear and doubt
don't have to win—God's truth is
stronger than any lie, and His peace
can overcome every fear.

For God has not given us a spirit of fear, but of
power, love, and a sound mind.

2 Timothy 1:7

Overcoming Fear and Doubt

Heavenly Father,
Fear and doubt often creep into my heart, leaving me overwhelmed, uncertain, and questioning my next steps. These feelings cloud my mind and make it difficult to see the truth of Your promises. But I know You have not given me a spirit of fear. You've given me power, love, and a sound mind.

In the name of Jesus Christ, I take authority over every fearful and doubting thought. I declare that fear and doubt have no place in my heart or my mind. I bind their influence and cast them out, replacing them with Your truth and Your peace.

Lord, surround me with the calm assurance that You are in control. Fill my heart with faith and remind me that Your plans for me are good, even when the path ahead feels unclear. Teach me to trust You fully, knowing that You are my protector, my strength, and my guide.

When fear arises, help me to focus on Your Word and stand firm in Your promises. Let Your Spirit strengthen me and give me boldness to face every challenge with confidence in Your power.

Thank You for being my shield, my refuge, and my unfailing hope. With You, I can face anything.
~*In Jesus' name, Amen.*

Surrendering to God's Will

Father,

When life feels uncertain and I don't know what's ahead, doubt fills my heart and makes me question Your plan. I want to trust You, but I often feel overwhelmed by what I don't understand. Yet I know You see the bigger picture—the details I cannot comprehend—and You are working all things for good.

Help me to release my need for control and to place my trust completely in You. Quiet the voices of doubt and anxiety that try to steal my peace, and fill my heart with the assurance that Your ways are higher than mine and Your timing is perfect.

Teach me to take each step in faith, even when I don't have all the answers. Show me that You are with me, guiding me, and preparing me for something greater than I could ever imagine. Help me to find joy in the journey, even when the road feels long or difficult.

Lord, give me the courage to trust You in every aspect of my life—my relationships, my work, and my future. Remind me daily that You hold my life in Your hands, and Your plans are always for my good.

Thank You for being faithful, for never leaving me, and for leading me with love.
~In Jesus' name, Amen.

Strength to Overcome Fear

Heavenly Father,

Fear often tries to stop me in my tracks, keeping me stuck in the "what-ifs" and the unknown. It makes me question my strength and whether I'm capable of moving forward. But I know You are my strength and my shield. With You, I can face anything.

Fill me with boldness and courage, Lord. Help me to stand firm in my faith, knowing that You are with me every step of the way. When fear tries to take hold of my heart, remind me of Your promises—that You will never leave me or forsake me, and that I can do all things through Christ who strengthens me.

Let Your Spirit fill my heart with peace and confidence, silencing the doubts and worries that try to creep in. Teach me to rely on Your strength instead of my own, trusting that Your power is made perfect in my weakness.

Lord, help me to see every challenge as an opportunity to grow closer to You. Strengthen my faith, and remind me that You are bigger than any obstacle I may face. With You by my side, I will walk in courage, knowing that Your plans for me are good.

Thank You for being my rock, my fortress, and my unwavering guide.
~In Jesus' name, Amen.

PHYSICAL AND EMOTIONAL HEALING

Pain—whether in your body or your heart—can make life feel unbearable. It can drain your strength, cloud your hope, and leave you wondering if healing is even possible. But God is still the Healer, and His power to restore is alive today.

He heals the brokenhearted and binds up their wounds.

Psalm 147:3

Healing from Illness

Lord Jesus,

You are the Great Healer, the One who spoke life into creation, restored the broken, and brought sight to the blind. Today, I bring my sickness and pain before You, trusting in Your power to restore me.

Strengthen my body, Lord, and breathe new life into every cell. Renew my energy and restore what has been broken. Let Your healing presence fill me from head to toe, driving out anything that is not from You. Speak life into every part of me that is weak, bringing wholeness and vitality where there has been sickness and pain.

Lord, as I wait for healing, give me patience and courage. In the moments when it feels far away, remind me of Your love and faithfulness. Let Your peace guard my heart and mind so I can rest in the assurance that You are with me every step of this journey.

Guide the hands of doctors and caregivers, and bless those who walk alongside me with compassion and understanding. Use this time to draw me closer to You and to deepen my faith in Your goodness.

Thank You for being my source of strength, my hope, and my healing. I trust You completely, Lord, and I place my body and spirit in Your hands.
~In Jesus' name, Amen.

Emotional Restoration

Lord,

My heart carries wounds that words cannot fully express. Past hurts, disappointments, and struggles weigh me down, leaving scars that I don't know how to heal. I try to move forward, but the pain lingers, and at times, it feels overwhelming. Yet I know that You see every part of me—the pain I hide, the tears I've cried, and the burdens I carry alone.

Come into those places, Lord, where my heart feels broken and bring healing where I need it most. Replace my sorrow with joy, my bitterness with forgiveness, and my fear with peace. Teach me to surrender my pain to You, knowing that You are the only one who can truly restore my heart and bring wholeness where I feel fractured.

Give me the courage to forgive those who have hurt me and to release the weight of anger and resentment. Fill the empty places in my heart with Your love, and remind me that I am never alone—You are always by my side, ready to comfort and guide me.

Thank You for being my refuge, my comforter, and the One who makes all things new. I place my trust in You, Lord, knowing that Your love has the power to heal every wound. ~ *In Jesus' name, Amen.*

Strength During Recovery

Heavenly Father,

Healing is a process, and I admit that sometimes I grow weary in the waiting. The road to recovery feels long and uncertain, and there are moments when my strength feels like it has run out. But I know that Your power is made perfect in my weakness, and I trust You to carry me through.

Help me to trust You in the process, even when I don't see progress. Teach me to be patient with myself and with the timing of Your work in my life. Renew my strength each day, and give me the perseverance to take one step at a time, trusting that You are working in ways I cannot see.

Surround me with Your peace, Lord, and help me to rest in the assurance that You are with me. Send people into my life who can encourage me, pray with me, and walk alongside me in this journey. Let every small victory remind me of Your faithfulness and give me hope for the future.

Thank You for being my constant support, my unshakable hope, and my refuge in times of difficulty. I trust in Your love and Your promises, and I look forward to the day when healing is complete.

~In Jesus' name, Amen.

RELATIONSHIP STRUGGLES

Conflict, betrayal, and distance in
relationships can leave you feeling
broken, unseen, and unworthy of love.
But God can restore what's been lost
and bring healing to even the deepest
wounds.

———————————— ✳ ————————————

Be kind to one another, tenderhearted,

forgiving one another, as God in Christ

forgave you.

Ephesians 4:32

Forgiveness and Reconciliation

Lord,

You see the brokenness in my relationships—the pain caused by misunderstandings, harsh words, and unresolved conflict. These wounds feel heavy, and sometimes it's hard to know how to move forward. But I know You are a God of reconciliation and healing, and nothing is beyond Your power to restore.

Teach me how to forgive, even when it feels impossible. Soften my heart and give me the courage to let go of resentment and bitterness. Replace those feelings with Your love, so I can see others as You see them. Help me to let go of my need to be right and to prioritize love and peace over pride.

Lord, I ask for wisdom in rebuilding trust where it has been broken. Show me how to take the first step toward reconciliation, trusting that You will guide the process. Heal the wounds that time alone cannot fix, and restore what has been lost in ways that only You can.

Teach me to love as You have loved me—with patience, grace, and a heart willing to forgive. Thank You for being the ultimate example of reconciliation through the cross, showing me that no relationship is too far gone for Your redemptive power.

~In Jesus' name, Amen.

Finding Balance in Relationships

Lord Jesus,

You have called us to love one another, but sometimes love feels complicated. I want to honor others and show kindness, but I often find it hard to balance that with protecting my heart. Teach me how to create healthy boundaries that reflect Your wisdom and love.

Help me to recognize when to say "yes" with compassion and when to say "no" with kindness. Give me discernment to guard my peace without shutting others out. Let my boundaries reflect a heart that honors You while respecting myself and others.

Lord, guide my relationships so that they are built on mutual respect, trust, and love. Help me to see the difference between relationships that draw me closer to You and those that drain my spirit. Give me the strength to walk away from unhealthy situations with grace and the courage to invest in relationships that honor You.

Teach me to love others in a way that reflects Your truth and goodness. Let my actions and decisions be grounded in Your Word, and help me to rely on Your Spirit for guidance. Thank You for being my example of perfect love, and for teaching me how to live with both grace and wisdom.

~In Jesus' name, Amen.

Strength to Move On

Lord,

Letting go is one of the hardest things You ask of us. When relationships end or change, it's easy to feel abandoned, confused, and afraid of what's next. But I trust that You see the bigger picture and that Your plans for me are good, even when I can't see them myself.

Help me to release what I cannot control and to place my trust fully in You. Give me the strength to let go of the past without losing hope for the future. Teach me to find peace in the knowledge that You are always working for my good, even in the midst of pain and uncertainty.

Lord, fill the empty spaces in my heart with Your love. Remind me that my worth is not found in any relationship but in You alone. When I feel weak or lonely, help me to turn to You for comfort and strength. Let Your Spirit fill me with the confidence to move forward boldly, knowing that You have already prepared the path ahead.

Thank You for walking with me every step of the way and for being my constant source of hope. I trust You to lead me into a new season filled with purpose, peace, and joy.

~In Jesus' name, Amen.

GENERATIONAL CURSES AND FAMILY STRUGGLES

Patterns of dysfunction in families can feel impossible to break. It's easy to feel trapped by the weight of past mistakes and generational struggles. But God's power is greater than any curse, and His love can bring healing and restoration to your family line.

The Lord is faithful to all generations.

Psalm 100:5

Breaking Curses

Lord,
I come to You in faith, declaring Your authority over my life. You are my Savior, Redeemer, and Protector, and by the power of Your cross, Your blood, and Your resurrection, I claim victory over every attack of the enemy.

In Your mighty name, I break the power of every curse, hex, spell, incantation, voodoo practice, witchcraft assignment, satanic ritual, or evil wish that has been spoken against me or passed through my generational bloodline. These forces have no authority here, and I command them to leave my life completely. Let every curse be rendered powerless and replaced with Your blessings and peace.

Lord, I renounce and ask forgiveness for any inner vows, agreements, or pacts I have made, knowingly or unknowingly, with the enemy. Break any bondages they have created in my life, and cover every area—my relationships, my work, my thoughts, and my future—with Your cleansing blood.

Thank You, Jesus, for surrounding me with Your love, for protecting me with Your angels, and for blessing me with Your grace and provision. I stand firm in the freedom You have won for me, trusting in Your power to guard and guide my life. *~ **In Jesus' name, Amen.***

Family Restoration

Heavenly Father,

You see the brokenness in my family—the misunderstandings, the hurts, and the distance that has grown between us over time. It's hard to face, but I know that nothing is beyond Your power to heal. You are a God of reconciliation, and I ask for Your healing hand to be upon us.

Bring forgiveness where there is bitterness, Lord. Let Your peace replace every conflict, and let Your love fill every space where division has taken hold. Soften our hearts and help us to see one another through Your eyes, with compassion, understanding, and grace.

Help us to break unhealthy patterns that have caused pain and to create new legacies rooted in faith, kindness, and unity. Show us how to speak words that build up rather than tear down and how to extend the same mercy to others that You have shown to us.

Lord, I trust You to restore what has been lost and to create something beautiful in its place. Reunite us in ways that only You can, and let Your presence be the foundation of our family. Thank You for Your endless love and faithfulness, which give me hope for the future.

~In Jesus' name, Amen.

Protection Over My Family

Heavenly Father,

I bring my family before You, trusting in Your love and care. You are our shield, our refuge, and our defender. Surround us with Your angels, guarding us from harm, illness, and danger—both seen and unseen.

Place a hedge of protection around our home, Lord. Let it be a place of peace and safety, filled with Your presence and love. Protect us from the enemy's schemes, from fear, and from anything that seeks to divide or discourage us. Let Your light dispel any darkness that tries to enter our hearts or home.

As we go about our daily lives, watch over us in every step we take. Keep us safe in our work, school, and travels. Guide us away from harm and temptation, and strengthen our faith to trust You in every situation.

Unite us as a family, Lord, in love and kindness. Teach us to encourage one another, to forgive freely, and to rely on You together. May Your blessings overflow in our lives, shining as a testimony of Your faithfulness.

Thank You for being our protector, our provider, and our strength. We rest in the assurance of Your unfailing love.

~In Jesus' name, Amen.

GRATITUDE
AND
RENEWAL

Even in the hardest times, there is a
reason to be thankful. Gratitude
reminds us of God's faithfulness, and
renewal refreshes us to keep moving
forward.

Give thanks in all circumstances; for this is
God's will for you in Christ Jesus.
1 Thessalonians 5:18

Thanksgiving for Freedom

Father,

Thank You for rescuing me and setting me free. You have carried me through the storms of life, broken the chains that once held me captive, and filled my heart with peace that only You can give. Your faithfulness, power, and unfailing love are beyond anything I could ever deserve, and I praise You for who You are.

Help me to live each day with a thankful heart, remembering all the ways You have worked in my life. Let my gratitude overflow into every part of my being, bringing joy to my spirit and encouragement to those around me. Teach me to recognize Your hand in both the small moments and the big victories, so that my life becomes a constant reflection of Your goodness.

Lord, remind me that my freedom is not just for my benefit, but to glorify You and to serve others with love and humility. Strengthen me to walk in the freedom You've given me, unburdened by fear or doubt. Let my gratitude be a daily act of worship, pointing others to Your power and grace.

You are my strength, my salvation, and my song. I give You all the glory now and forever.

~In Jesus' name, Amen.

Renewal Through the Holy Spirit

Holy Spirit,

Breathe fresh life into my weary soul. Fill me with Your peace where there has been restlessness, Your joy where there has been sadness, and Your strength where I have felt weak and uncertain.

Renew my heart, Lord, and help me to release the burdens I've been carrying for too long. Teach me to let go of the things I cannot control and to trust in Your perfect timing and wisdom. Fill me with the confidence to trust You more deeply, and help me to step boldly into the plans You have for me.

Let Your Spirit flow through me, bringing hope, healing, and a renewed passion for Your purpose in my life. Empower me to face each day with courage and faith, knowing that You are working in and through me. Transform the broken places in my heart into places of beauty, and remind me that You never give up on me, even when I fall short.

Thank You for Your unending grace, Your patience, and Your power to make all things new. Help me to reflect Your love to others, so that my renewal becomes a testimony of Your goodness.

~In Jesus' name, Amen.

Joy in Difficult Times

Heavenly Father,

Even when life feels hard, I know You are my refuge and strength. Your presence gives me hope and reminds me that joy is not dependent on my circumstances—it is rooted in who You are and the promises You've made.

Teach me to find joy even in the struggles, to see Your blessings in the midst of trials, and to hold fast to Your Word when I feel discouraged. Let Your promises fill my heart with peace and assurance, reminding me that You are always working for my good, even when I cannot see the full picture.

Lord, show me how to focus on Your faithfulness, no matter what I face. Help me to notice the small ways You are at work in my life and to celebrate Your goodness in every season. Let Your joy carry me through every trial, giving me the strength to endure and the courage to keep moving forward.

Thank You for being my unshakable foundation, my source of hope, and the giver of true and lasting joy. I trust in Your goodness and rest in the assurance that You are with me, always.

~In Jesus' name, Amen.

HEALING
THROUGH
REFLECTION

There are moments when the weight
of what we carry feels too heavy, and
the only way forward is to release it
into God's hands. Through reflection
and prayer, healing begins.

Cast all your anxiety on him because he
cares for you.
1 Peter 5:7

Healing Through Reflection

Life can leave its mark on our hearts—disappointments, broken relationships, and unspoken struggles that weigh heavily on us. These burdens can keep us from fully experiencing the peace and freedom God desires for us.

Writing a prayerful letter is a way to bring these struggles before the Lord, releasing what has been holding you back and inviting His healing presence into your life.

Through this exercise, you'll take a step toward healing by surrendering your struggles into God's hands and trusting Him to make all things new.

How to Write Your Healing Prayer Letter

Begin with Prayer
Ask God to reveal any unresolved pain or relationships that need healing. Pray for courage, honesty, and the guidance of the Holy Spirit as you begin.

Example prayer:

"Lord, I come to You with a heavy heart. Show me the areas in my life where I need healing and the people I need to forgive. Help me to see these situations through Your eyes, and give me the courage to release my pain into Your hands."

Write with Honesty

Picture the person or situation that caused you pain and write directly to them, even if they will never see this letter. Express your feelings honestly—whether it's anger, sadness, confusion, or regret. Don't worry about how it sounds; this is between you and God.

Example opening:
"I feel hurt because…" or *"I was angry when…"*

This step is about releasing what has been weighing you down. Acknowledge the emotions you've carried and the impact the situation has had on your heart and mind.

Invite God into the Process

Once you've expressed your feelings, shift your focus to God. Ask Him to help you release your pain and forgive those who have hurt you. Surrender the situation into His hands, trusting in His ability to heal what is broken.

Example transition:
"Lord, I give this pain to You. I ask for Your healing in this area of my life and for the strength to let go of the anger and hurt I've carried."

End with Hope and Gratitude

Close your letter by reflecting on God's promises and expressing gratitude for His faithfulness. Thank Him for the healing that is already taking place and the peace that comes from trusting Him.

Example closing:
"Thank You, Lord, for lifting this burden from my heart. I trust that You are working in my life, bringing healing and restoration. I praise You for Your love and faithfulness, which never fail."

What to Do Next

When you've finished writing, spend time in prayer over your letter. If you feel led, you can keep it as a reminder of the healing process or destroy it as a symbolic act of releasing the pain to God.

This exercise is not about the other person—it's about your heart and your relationship with God. You can repeat it as often as needed, trusting that each step brings you closer to the freedom and peace He offers.

THANK YOU

At Faithstone, we are honored to be part of your spiritual journey. Thank you for choosing this prayer book as a tool to deepen your connection with God. We pray that these words bring you comfort, strength, and renewal in every season of life.

We'd love to continue supporting your faith journey. Visit our website at **Faithstone.org** to discover more of our faith-based products designed to uplift and inspire. From devotionals to spiritual tools, we're here to walk alongside you.

And don't forget—you have access to **free audio version of the prayers** from this book. These guided prayers are available anytime, anywhere to bring you peace and encouragement May God's love and peace surround you always.

Thank you for allowing Faithstone to be part of your walk with Christ.

Acknowledgments

Faithstone extends appreciation to the centuries of believers who have safeguarded and shared public-domain prayers and scriptures.

Among these revered contributions are the Anima Christi, Psalm 91, and other longstanding devotions that have guided many souls toward hope and renewal.

Their resonance echoes through history, and this publication upholds that heritage by including such texts for modern reflection.

Faithstone acknowledges these sources with the utmost respect, recognizing their continued power to nurture faith in every generation.